# BREAK

# PRAYER

## 90 Days of Supernatural Breakthrough & Open Heavens

## UBACUS ALPHONSE

Ubacus Alphonse
Cressland, Soufriere
St. Lucia, West Indies
ubacus@hotmail.com

Printed in the United States of America
Createspace Publishing Company

© Copyright 2017 –Ubacus Alphonse
ISBN-13: 978-1530304875
ISBN-10: 1530304873

## DEDICATION

This powerful prayer manual is designed for all those seeking an accelerated turnaround in life. This powerful ninety (90) day declarations for breakthrough is a guide to receive the blessings which are rightfully yours through a life of complete trust and obedience through the promises of God's word.

**Though your beginning was small, yet your latter end would increase abundantly.**

**Job 8:7**

## ACKNOWLEDGMENTS

Almighty God for his grace and mercy in giving me the strength to compile this prayer book which I believe will be a tremendous blessing to you.

## BEFORE YOU BEGIN

I want to thank you wholeheartedly for purchasing a copy of this book. In your hands are powerful prayers designed to bring accelerated breakthrough in every area of your life. This is your divine season to receive God's provision of peace, healing, prosperity, deliverance and restoration in every area of your life.

You were not meant to live in defeat, poverty, setback and adversity. Christ died so that you and I could enjoy and be partakers of his divine blessings. You have an inheritance in Christ Jesus and it is time to take possession of your inheritance as a child of God. (Romans 8:17)

As you release these prayers in faith, you must believe and have the confidence that God is able to turn your situation around.

These prayers must be prayed with a measure of fervent faith and aggression against the powers of darkness. You must decide whether you want to be free or whether you want to continue languishing under the weights and burdens of the devil which will bring only destruction.

I declare that your latter shall be greater than what you have been through in the past. I prophesy increase in every area of your life. I declare that success, prosperity, good health, wisdom and understanding is yours in this season.

Whatever the enemy has devoured in your life shall be restored to you one hundredfold in this season. Receive your supernatural breakthrough and open heaven in this season in the mighty name of Jesus Christ.

Be Blessed!!

This prayer manual is a tool to be utilized by born again believers. You cannot be living in sin and declaring war on the enemy. Your life will only result in further bombardments by the enemy because the root of sin, rebellion and disobedience has not been dealt with. This manual should not be used as a tool to attack anyone rather a guide to enhance your prayer life.

**If you don't know Jesus Christ as Lord and personal Savior please pray the following prayer with all seriousness before proceeding through the pages of this book.**

## PRAYER OF SALVATION

Father in Heaven, I admit that I am a sinner and I ask Your forgiveness for living a life of sin and walking in constant disobedience to Your word. Thank You for sending Your son Jesus Christ to die on the cross for my sins so that I can be redeemed from the hands of the devil. Even now, I accept Your Son Jesus Christ as my Lord and personal Savior and I thank You for cleansing me with Your precious blood. Father, You said in 1 John 1:9 "If we confess our sins, You are faithful and just and will forgive us our sins and purify us from all unrighteousness." Thank You for breaking the yoke of bondage over my life and setting me free from the captivity of the enemy. Thank You for restoration and complete deliverance in my mind, heart, spirit, soul and body. In Jesus' Mighty Name. Amen!

## PRAYER OF FORGIVENESS

**Unforgiveness can also hinder your prayers from being answered. Therefore it is very important that you close the doors of bitterness, hatred and unforgiveness.**

Father in Heaven, I ask Your forgiveness for opening my life to the spirit of bitterness, hatred and unforgiveness. Even now I choose to forgive the person/s who have hurt me and I close the door and I give no place to the devil in my life. I pray that You would cover me with Your precious blood and even now I choose to love my enemies as You have commanded. I receive Your love even now and I choose to reciprocate this love to others. In Jesus Mighty Name. Amen.

## BASIC REQUIREMENTS BEFORE USING THIS PRAYER MANUAL

1. You must be born again. You must repent of every sin in your life and surrender your life over to the Lordship of Jesus Christ. You must ensure that you close all doors opened to the enemy through sin and give no place to the devil. **I wish to state emphatically that you cannot be living in sin and declaring war on Satan at the same time. You are doing yourself more harm than good. Get out of the life of sin and repent.**

2. Forgive everyone who has hurt you or caused you pain in the past. Unforgiveness can hinder your deliverance and

prayer from being heard. Let go of the past, close all open doors and embrace the future Christ has marked out for you.

3. Strive to live a Holy life and humble yourself before the Lord that He may lift you up. Surrender your life fully and be obedient to the Word of God and the leading of the Holy Spirit.

4. Clean out your house- go through your home and remove every cursed object or anything known to give demons the legal right to stay there. Burn all satanic books, literature, religious objects, horse shoes, etc. Anoint the doors, windows and rooms with olive oil and declare "I cover and seal this house with the precious blood of Jesus and command every demonic spirits that has attached itself to this place to leave now in the Mighty Name of Jesus Christ.

5. Be faithful in your prayers and fasting and command every demonic spirit affecting your life to flee. Invite the Holy Spirit to take control of your life.

6. Continue to walk in freedom and study the Word of God so that you can mature spiritually. Get a good bible teaching church and continue to grow spiritually.

## CLOSING DOORWAYS TO THE ENEMY

Demonic spirits operate in the lives of the unbeliever through demonic doorways. These are the legal gateways or entry points which the devil has been given by you to operate in your life legally. As long as you have opened a door to the enemy, you give the devil a legal right to be there. It is important that you close all doors through sin which you have given to the enemy knowingly or unknowingly and shut the access points.

**Demonic spirits enter our lives through the following doorways:**

1. Generational curses
2. Occult activities
3. Unforgiveness
4. Sexual perversion
5. Ungodly soul ties

## STEPS TO CLOSING DEMONIC DOORWAYS

1. Identify the open doors in your life
2. Repent and ask God to forgive you of your sins
3. Commit to walking in holiness before God
4. Meditate on God's Word and keep the door of sin closed.

## Breakthrough Declaration 1

*See, I have this day set you over the nations and over the kingdoms, to root out and to pull down, to destroy and to throw down, to build and to plant.*

*Jeremiah 1:9-11*

---

**H**eavenly Father, I thank you for this great assignment which you have given to me here on earth. I thank you that by the power of your Holy Spirit and your anointing, I am empowered to root out, pull down, destroy, build and plant. I declare from my position of authority that I root out, pull down and destroy the plans and assignments of the demonic forces of darkness concerning my life, my church, my nation, my family, health, marriage and finances this year in the mighty Name of Jesus Christ.

I declare that the kingdoms of this world has become the kingdom of our Lord and of his Christ, and He shall reign forever and ever. I declare the Lordship of Christ rules and reigns over the territorial atmosphere of my home, ministry and nation in the mighty name of Jesus Christ.

I command angels on assignment to war against the forces of evil seeking to destroy, sabotage and frustrate the destiny of the children of God in the Mighty Name of Jesus Christ. **Amen.**

### CONFESSION

I am anointed by God to defeat the forces of darkness. I declare that I rule and reign with Christ. I am victorious. I cannot be defeated this year.

## Breakthrough Declaration 2

*Tell the righteous it will be well with them, for they will enjoy the fruit of their deeds. Woe to the wicked! Disaster is upon them! They will be paid back for what their hands have done.*

*Isaiah 3:10-11*

---

**H**eavenly Father, I decree and declare that it shall be well with me this year. I declare that it shall be well with my family. It shall be well with my finances. It shall be well with my children. It shall be well with my health. It shall be well with my marriage. It shall be well with my ministry in the mighty Name of Jesus Christ. I declare that the wicked shall reap what they have sown in the mighty Name of Jesus. Thank you Father, for delivering my life and my family from the plans of wicked men this year in the Name of Jesus Christ. From the beginning of this year to the end of the year, goodness, mercy, and favour shall follow me in the matchless name of Jesus Christ. **Amen.**

## CONFESSION

I will not be afraid because the Lord has promised that it shall be well with me. I will find rest, peace and safety in the Lord. The lot of the wicked shall be disaster, but I will enjoy the fruits of my deeds.

## Breakthrough Declaration 3

*For He shall give His angels charge over you, to keep you in all your ways. In their hands they shall bear you up, Lest you dash your foot against a stone.*

*Psalm 91:11-12*

---

**H**eavenly Father, thank You that this year the angels of the Lord are watching over me and my family to preserve us from very demonic plan, plot, assignment and satanic agenda of the enemy. I thank you that the angels of the Lord are watching over me, my family, my house, my children, my car, my business, my workplace and everything else that belongs to me or is connected to me in the Name of Jesus Christ. I declare that this year those who wage war against me and my family will be ashamed because the Lord is my defense. The Lord is my strength, my shield and my helper. The Lord is my rock, my fortress, my deliverer and my buckler. Behold all those who are angered against me will surely be ashamed and confounded. The wicked shall perish, and the enemies of the Lord shall be as the fat of lambs. They shall be consumed in the Name of Jesus. **Amen.**

### CONFESSION

I declare that the angels of the Lord are with me. I declare that warring angels with flaming swords of fire shall surround me and my family this year.

## Breakthrough Declaration 4

*Being confident of this very thing, that He who has begun a good work in you will complete it until the day of Jesus Christ.*

**Philippians 1:6**

---

**H**eavenly Father, I am confident of this very thing, that He who has begun a good work in me will complete it until the day of Jesus Christ. I declare the good work which Christ has started in me shall be completed in my life. I cancel every plan, plot, assignment or attempt of the enemy to take me out of the will of God for my life, ministry and destiny. I release warring angels with flaming swords of fire to fight against every demonic strongman hindering the will of God for my life. I declare that this year the floodgates of heaven are opened over my life in the Name of Jesus. I declare favor, goodness and mercy are going before me I declare the presence of the Lord is with me. I command demonic assignments of stagnancy, procrastination and limitation to be broken from my life this year in the Name of Jesus Christ of Nazareth. Thank You Lord for hearing and answering my prayers. **Amen.**

## CONFESSION

I declare that this year my ministry shall be fulfilled. My destiny shall be fulfilled. My calling shall be fulfilled. My life shall be preserved until the day of our Lord Jesus Christ.

## Breakthrough Declaration 5

*For surely there is a hereafter, and your hope will not be cut off.*

*Proverbs 23:18*

---

**H**eavenly Father, thank you that this year, there is a future hope for me, and my hope will not be cut off in the Name of Jesus. I declare that I have a glorious hope in Christ. I declare that with this hope I shall be confident in what the Lord shall do in my life this year. I declare that I shall not be moved by the circumstances and situations which the devil will send into my life this year. I shall stand in the faith and confidence of my God. I declare the doors of heavenly treasures are opened to me in the Name of Jesus. I declare open heavens over my life, family, business, job, marriage and ministry in the Name of Jesus. I thank you Lord that my hope will not be cut off in the Name of Jesus Christ. **Amen.**

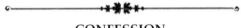

### CONFESSION

I have a secured hope in Christ. I have an eternal hope in Christ. I have a glorious hope in Christ. My future is bright in Christ. I have an expected hope that will not be cut off. The plans of God for my life is to give me a hope and a future. I place my hope, trust and confidence in the hope and future which Christ has promised for my life and destiny.

14

## Breakthrough Declaration 6

*Therefore we also, since we are surrounded by so great a cloud of witnesses, let us lay aside every weight, and the sin which so easily ensnares us, and let us run with endurance the race that is set before us, looking unto Jesus, the author and finisher of our faith.*

*Hebrews 12:1-2*

Heavenly Father, I lay aside every weight and the sin which so easily ensnares us and I run with patience the race which is set before me. I declare that this year I am laying down everything in my life which seeks to entangle me and keep me in bondage to the vices of the enemy. I declare that I run with patience, persistence and endurance the race which is set before and I look up to Jesus who is the author and the finisher of my faith. I will forget those things which are behind and reach forward to what lies ahead in the Name of Jesus. **Amen.**

### CONFESSION

I am free from sin, entanglements and everything which hinders my walk with the Lord. I declare that my eyes are on the Lord and I am moving forward with patience and endurance. I declare that the past is behind me and I am moving forward with my future secured in Christ.

## Breakthrough Declaration 7

*No weapon formed against you shall prosper, And every tongue which rises against you in judgment You shall condemn. This is the heritage of the servants of the Lord, and their righteousness is from Me," Says the Lord.*

*Isaiah 54:17*

**H**eavenly Father, I declare that no weapon that is formed or fashioned against me and my family shall prosper this year in the Mighty Name of Jesus Christ. I nullify every attack of the enemy concerning my life and my family this year in the Name of Jesus. I fire back to the senders every evil arrow of sickness, infirmity, disease, untimely death, tragedy and accidents in the Name of Jesus Christ. I cover my children and my family under the blood of Jesus and I thank You Lord for Your promise of divine protection. I command every curse, jinx, incantation, ritual and evil prayers sent against me and my family this year to be dismantled in the Mighty Name of Jesus Christ. **Amen.**

### CONFESSION

I am walking under the banner of victory, protection and freedom which Christ won for me when he purchased my salvation. I declare the banner of victory is over my life and my family. I declare I am walking under the banner of the blood of Jesus. I am an overcomer this year and all the days of my life here on this earth.

## Breakthrough Declaration 8

*I know your works, that you are neither cold nor hot. I could wish you were cold or hot. So then, because you are lukewarm, and neither cold nor hot, I will vomit you out of My mouth.*

*Revelations 3:15-16*

---

**H**eavenly Father, this year I annihilate every worldly spirit which shall seek to cause me to backslide in the Mighty Name of Jesus Christ. I declare that this year I will not backslide in the Name of Jesus but I will continue to grow in the grace and knowledge of our Lord and Savior Jesus Christ. I declare that my love for God shall not grow cold but I shall burn with the fire of his Holy Spirit and do great and mighty exploits for God. I pray Lord that this year I will continue to hunger and thirst for you. I pray that i would experience in this season a higher dimension of your presence and glory in my life. I pray Lord that you fill my cup and let it overflow until I thirst no more. **Amen.**

### CONFESSION

I declare that I am on fire with the love of God. My life is being transformed every single day. I declare that I shall not be lukewarm but my life will burn with fire, passion and a sincere desire for the kingdom of God.

## Breakthrough Declaration 9

*Trust in the Lord, and do good; dwell in the land, and feed on His faithfulness.*

*Psalm 37:3*

---

**H**eavenly **Father,** I declare that this year, I will experience the goodness and divine favor of the Lord. I come against every spirit of lack in the Name of Jesus. I decree and declare open doors of favor, open doors of opportunity, open doors of advancement, open doors of promotion, open doors of business opportunity, open doors of ministry, open doors of employment, open doors of abundance in the Name of Jesus Christ. I declare that this year the doors which has been closed against my life shall be opened in the name of Jesus. I will trust in the Lord at all times because he is my hope, confidence and rewarder. I declare that I will feed on his faithfulness for He is the strength of my life. **Amen.**

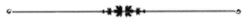

### CONFESSION

I declare that this year I am waking into a season of multiplied blessings. Nobody can stop the plans and purpose of God for my life and destiny because I am a blessed, chosen and favored child of Almighty God. Doors of favor and multiplied blessings shall be opened and no devil in hell can stop it.

## Breakthrough Declaration 10

*Yea, though I walk through the valley of the shadow of death, I will fear no evil; For You are with me; Your rod and Your staff, they comfort me.*

*Psalm 23:4*

---

**H**eavenly Father, I declare that though I walk through the valley of the shadow of death this year, I will fear no evil for you are with me. I thank you that Your rod and Your staff they comfort me. I decree and declare that this year I will not be afraid. I will not fear because God has not given to me a spirit of fear. I will walk in the faith and confidence of my God knowing that He is the God who is able to do what man cannot do. I pray that as I study Your word and meditate upon Your precious promises, You will prosper me like the tree planted besides streams of water. Goodness and mercy shall follow me and I shall dwell in the house of the Lord forever, for my eyes have seen the goodness of the Lord. This year shall be a turning point in my life and the years ahead of me. **Amen.**

## CONFESSION

I shall not be afraid. My faith and confidence in God is bigger than my fears. I trust a big God who is able to do great and mighty things for me. I will prosper like the tree planted besides the streams of water.

## Breakthrough Declaration 11

*And Jabez called on the God of Israel saying,*
*"Oh, that You would bless me indeed, and*
*enlarge my territory, that Your hand would*
*be with me, and that You would keep me*
*from evil, that I may not cause pain!" So*
*God granted him what he requested.*

*1 Chronicles 4:10*

**H**eavenly Father, I declare that this year, like Jabez, the Lord will expand my territory. I declare enlargement both spiritually and physically. I declare this year I will be a blessing to those around me. Thank You Lord that I will be blessed to be a blessing. Let Your hand be with me and Your presence go before me. Let Your hand be upon my family, my children, my marriage, my business, my job, my career, my ministry, my coming out and my going in, in the Mighty Name of Jesus Christ. I decree and declare that this year my life will not be a source of pain but a source of blessing in the Mighty Name of Jesus Christ. I pray that you restore all that the locusts and cankerworm has eaten so that I may praise your name for you have dealt with me wondrously. **Amen.**

### CONFESSION

My life is not a product of lack, defeat or adversity. I am
blessed to be a blessing. No curse or poverty shall cling to
my life because in Christ, I am rich and not poor. I am
blessed and not cursed. I am strong and not weak.

## Breakthrough Declaration 12

*Then the Lord said to me, "You have seen well, for I am ready to perform My word.*

*Jeremiah 1:12*

H eavenly Father, thank you that you are watching over your word to perform it in my life. I pray that this year all my enemies who are watching, planning, organizing, strategizing and executing desires for evil shall be put to shame in the Name of Jesus. I decree and declare by the power of Almighty God that the satanic plans, plots and assignments of the enemy concerning my life this year shall blow up their faces in the Name of Jesus. I declare that the Word of God shall stand above every word of the adversary in my life in the Name of Jesus. I decree and declare that God is opening doors of opportunities for me and I boldly step into them. I will not relent neither will I hold back. I will be all that God wants me to be. I shall increase in strength. With the arrows of the Lord, I shall strike down my enemies. I will not grow weary till I have gained victory over them in the name of Jesus. **Amen.**

### CONFESSION

The word of God is greater than any other word spoken in my life by people and satanic enemies who desire to destroy my life through curses and spells. The word of man shall fail but the word of God shall prevail over my life and my adversaries.

21

## Breakthrough Declaration 13

*Though your beginning was small, yet your latter end would increase abundantly.*

*Job 8:7*

---

**H**eavenly Father, thank you that my latter shall be greater than my past. I decree and declare by the power of God that this year shall be my best and most blessed year in the Name of Jesus Christ. I thank You Lord that in the midst of difficulties and challenges of life; Your hand will guide me, lead me, sustain me and protect me from all harm of the enemy. Though my beginning was small, I thank you that because of Your great faithfulness, my latter end will increase abundantly. I thank You Father that this year is my year of laughter and unspeakable joy. Though the enemy wants to reduce me to tears, I thank You that the joy of the Lord will be my strength through the challenges and difficulties of this life. I refuse to bow and suffer defeat at the hands of the enemy this year in the Name of Jesus. **Amen.**

### CONFESSION

This year shall be my best year and my most blessed year. I declare that I shall see the goodness of the Lord in my life, family, marriage, ministry, finances, business and career this year. My life shall be blessed.

## Breakthrough Declaration 14

*Be diligent to present yourself approved to God, a worker who does not need to be ashamed, rightly dividing the word of truth.*

*2 Timothy 2:15*

---

**H**eavenly Father, I declare that this year I will study to show myself approved unto God. I declare that I walk in holiness and righteousness and I will pursue God like never before. This year I will become a prayer eagle. I will arise in prayer with the wings of the eagles over my adversaries and trample upon every plan of the enemy concerning my life this year. I will wrestle with God in prayer like Jacob wrestled with God. I decree and declare this year I refuse to lose sight of my purpose, calling, ministry and my destiny in the Name of Jesus Christ. **Amen.**

## CONFESSION

I will arise and pursue God in prayer. I will pursue a higher
dimension of prayer. A higher dimension of fasting. A
higher dimension of his presence in my life. I will wrestle
with God this year and refuse to let him go until he blesses
me.

## Breakthrough Declaration 15

*I am the Alpha and the Omega, the Beginning and the End, "says the Lord, who is and who was and who is to come, the Almighty."*

*Revelation 1:8*

---

**H**eavenly Father, I declare that You are the Alpha and the Omega, the God of the beginning and the end. I pray that the good work which You have started in my life shall come to fruition this year in the Name of Jesus Christ. I prophesy that my life shall have a good ending in the Name of Jesus. I prophesy health, strength and long life in the mighty Name of Jesus Christ. I declare my latter shall be greater than my past. I speak to every problem, circumstance, and situation and command them to line up with the Word of God in the Name of Jesus Christ. The Lord shall make me a sign and a wonder. I shall slay giants, break barriers and influence the nations by the mighty hand of God. **Amen.**

### CONFESSION

God is able to do all things in my life. If he started the good work in my life then he is able to complete it. I look upon him as the Author and the Finisher of my faith.

## Breakthrough Declaration 16

*He shall be like a tree planted by the rivers of water, that brings forth its fruit in its season, whose leaf also shall not wither; and whatever he does shall prosper.*

*Psalm 1:3*

---

**H**eavenly **Father,** I declare that this year I shall be like a tree planted by the rivers of water, which spreads out its roots by the river, and whatsoever I do shall prosper in the Name of Jesus. The glory of the Lord shall be revealed in my life and all flesh shall see it together, for the mouth of the Lord hath spoken it. The grass withered and the flower faded, but the word of my God shall stand forever in my life. Lord, I pray that You will send me dew and rain of favor and blessings. Lord, I thank You that You shall make me increase and my blessings shall not be denied in Jesus' Mighty Name. **Amen.**

## CONFESSION

I am like a tree planted by the waters. My roots are firm, fixed and strong in the Lord. Everything that I do shall prosper. The Word of God shall stand in my life and I shall be blessed with the dew of God's favor and multiplied blessings.

## Breakthrough Declaration 17

*I And make the crooked place straight;*
*I will break in pieces the gates of*
*bronze and cut the bars of iron.*

*Isaiah 45:2*

Heavenly Father, thank You that the gates of brass and iron which have imprisoned my potentials and caged my destiny shall be broken this year in the Mighty Name of Jesus. I thank you Father that my crooked places are being made straight. I thank you Father for breaking in pieces the gates of bronze and cutting the bars of iron. I thank You Father that my gates shall be opened continually to receive bountiful blessings. They shall not be shut day and night so that men may bring unto me the forces of the Gentiles and the wealth of the wicked in the Name of Jesus. I command any power that has held me captive to be broken in the name of Jesus. Arise in my life oh Lord and let every enemy be scattered in the matchless name of Jesus Christ.

### CONFESSION

My life and destiny shall not be caged. My potentials shall not be caged. My life shall make progress. The wealth of the wicked shall be laid up for the righteous.

## Breakthrough Declaration 18

*The steps of a good man are ordered by
the Lord, and He delights in his way.*
*Psalm 37:23*

**H**eavenly Father, I declare that this year my steps will always be guided by the mighty enabling hand of Almighty God. May every step I take this year lead me further and further into greater intimacy with You. Lord, I pray that You order my steps and establish me according to Your word. I command my blessings, finances, success, breakthrough, progress and favor to manifest this year in the mighty name of Jesus Christ. I declare that I am the head and not the tail, above and not beneath. Because the Lord is with me my life will make progress this year in the name of Jesus. I declare that I am destined to be great, I am destined to progress, I am destined to fulfill my calling and potential, I am destined for great and mighty things in God. Because the Lord is with me the devices of the enemy shall fail in the name of Jesus. I break the curse of backwardness, delay and procrastination over my life in the name of Jesus. Thank You Heavenly Father for going before me and establishing my steps this year. **Amen.**

### CONFESSION
I am a righteous man. My steps are established by the Lord.
He delights in my way.

## Breakthrough Declaration 19

*And they overcame him by the blood of the Lamb and by the word of their testimony, and they did not love their lives to the death.*

*Revelation 12:11*

---

**H**eavenly Father, I declare that in this season, I overcome the enemy by the power in the blood of Jesus and the word of my testimony. I thank you for delivering me from the bondage of the devil and destroying the power of the devil over my life this year. Lord, I pray for an overcoming spirit over every power of darkness. Lord, may I fight the good fight of faith and hold on to Your eternal Word until we come to the end of life's journey. I declare I am shielded under the banner of the blood of Jesus. I declare the blood before me, the blood above me, the blood in my going out and my coming in, the blood upon those I will encounter today, the blood upon my house and my business, the blood upon my vehicles, the blood upon my children and I speak the blood against every evil device of the enemy.

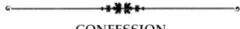

### CONFESSION

I have victory in the power of the blood of Jesus and my testimony. I am delivered by the power in the blood of Jesus. I have an overcoming spirit by the power in the blood of Jesus and the word of my testimony. My testimony is a powerful weapon to change lives and influence souls for the kingdom of God.

## Breakthrough Declaration 20

*The Lord is my light and my salvation; Whom shall I fear? The Lord is the strength of my life; of whom shall I be afraid?*

**Psalm 27:1**

---

**H**eavenly Father, I declare that this year the Lord shall be my light and my salvation. I will not fear for the Lord is with me. I declare that the Lord is the strength of my life. I will not be afraid for the Lord is with me to give me victory over the forces of darkness and my enemies. I declare that I will stand still and see the salvation and victory of the Lord over the wicked this year in the mighty Name of Jesus Christ. I cancel every expectation of the enemy concerning my life this year in the Mighty Name of Jesus Christ. May every secret and open enemy fighting against me this year be disgraced in the Name of Jesus Christ.

### CONFESSION

I am not afraid of what this year will bring because the Lord is the strength of my life. I will not be afraid of the future or wicked people who seek to rise up against me because the Lord is with me and has promised to give me victory.

## Breakthrough Declaration 21

*Blessed is the man who fears the Lord, Who delights greatly in His commandments. His descendants will be mighty on earth; The generation of the upright will be blessed. Wealth and riches will be in his house, and his righteousness endures forever.*

*Psalm 112:1-3*

---

**H**eavenly Father, I declare that I am blessed because I walk in the fear of the Lord and I delight greatly in his commandments. I declare that this year I purpose my life to fear the Lord and to walk in his ways. I declare that my descendants will be mighty in the earth. I proclaim that my children and my grandchildren shall be mighty in the earth. They shall serve the Lord and do great and mighty exploits for the Lord. I declare that the generation of the upright shall be blessed. Wealth and riches shall be in my house. I prophesy that this year there shall be no lack in the mighty Name of Jesus. I cancel every assignment and plan of the enemy to keep me from my destiny in the mighty Name of Jesus Christ. **Amen.**

## CONFESSION

I am blessed. I fear the Lord. I am delighting myself in the Lord and walking according to his ways. My generation shall be blessed in the earth. They shall be strong and mighty. My house is filled with riches. There is no scarcity.

## Breakthrough Declaration 22

*Your word is a lamp to my feet and a
light to my path.*

*Psalm 119:105*

---

**H**eavenly Father, thank You that Your Word is a lamp unto my feet and a light unto my path. I declare that this year the Word of the Lord will lead me and guide me into all truth. I purpose in my heart to walk in the ways of the Lord all 365 days of this year. I declare that as I walk in the ways of the Lord my life shall be prosperous. I decree and declare that this is my year of possibilities. I speak to every strongman or mountain in my life and I render them powerless and command them to fall and die under the power of God. Every flood that is lifted up against me shall be silenced in the name of Jesus. I shall not be swept away! **Amen.**

## CONFESSION

The Word of the Lord is my direction in life. When I don't know where to turn for help I will look to the Word of the Lord to lead me and guide my life through this life. The Word of the Lord is like a compass which leads me in the path of holiness and righteousness all the days of my life.

## Breakthrough Declaration 23

*For the weapons of our warfare are not carnal but mighty in God for pulling down strongholds, casting down arguments and every high thing that exalts itself against the knowledge of God, bringing every thought into captivity to the obedience of Christ.*

*2 Corinthians 10:4-5*

---

**H**eavenly Father, I declare that the weapons of my warfare are not carnal, but mighty in God for pulling down strongholds. casting down arguments and every high thing that exalts itself against the knowledge of God, bringing every thought into captivity to the obedience of Christ, and being ready to punish all disobedience when my obedience is fulfilled. He who sits in the heavens shall laugh; The Lord scoffs at the plans of the enemy. No divination or sorcery spoken against me shall stand. No curse shall touch me because I am blessed of the Lord. Whom the Lord has blessed no one can curse. **Amen.**

### CONFESSION

I exercise my weapons of victory against the forces of the enemy coming against my family, marriage, finances, children and destiny. Every stronghold in my life shall be broken and destroyed because of the power in the blood of Jesus.

## Breakthrough Declaration 24

*Open my eyes, that I may see wondrous things from Your law*

*Psalm 119:18*

---

Heavenly Father, I pray that you would open my eyes that I might see and behold the wondrous things from your word. I declare that this year I will not be bound by deception and the spirit of religion. Open my eyes Lord to the truth of your word which brings salvation, deliverance, healing and restoration. Free me Lord from unbelief and lack of faith in activating the word of God upon my life. Open my heart Lord that I might receive the full benefits of your word. Open my mind that I might meditate on your word day and night. Thank you Father that the eyes of my unsaved loved ones and family members are opened to receive the message of salvation and the yoke of the powers of darkness is broken over their lives. **Amen.**

### CONFESSION

My eyes are opened to the wondrous truth from the word of God. I am not blind for I walk by faith in the power of the Holy Spirit and His anointing. My mind and spirit is illuminated with truth from the word of God.

## Breakthrough Declaration 25

*He who sins is of the devil, for the devil has sinned from the beginning. For this purpose the Son of God was manifested, that He might destroy the works of the devil.*

*1 John 3:8*

---

**H**eavenly **Father**, thank you that it was for this purpose Jesus Christ was manifested to destroy the works of the devil. I thank you Father that the plans and works of the powers of darkness concerning my life this year is broken and destroyed. I declare the victory of Christ triumphs over every area of my life. I declare I am walking in total and complete victory in my life because Christ became a curse so that I can be blessed. I declare the blessings of Abraham are mine. I declare that the blessings of Christ are mine and I walk and enjoy this same victory today in Christ Jesus. **Amen.**

### CONFESSION

I am walking in dominion authority because of the finished work of Jesus Christ at the cross of Calvary. I rest in his victory over the powers of darkness.

## Breakthrough Declaration 26

*You are of God, little children, and have*
*overcome them, because He who is in you*
*is greater than he who is in the world.*

*1 John 4:4*

---

**H**eavenly Father, thank You, for overcoming victory over the powers of the enemy. I declare Heavenly Father, that greater is he that is in me than he that is in the world. I declare that Jesus Christ who is the Greater One lives in me. I declare that I am more than a conqueror in Christ Jesus. I declare that as a Child of the Most High God, I have overcome the plans and forces of the powers of darkness this year. The plans and purposes of God for my life shall prevail. No devil in hell shall be able to stop the will of God from coming into fruition in my life. The works of evil shall be destroyed but the plans and purpose of God concerning my life, future and destiny shall be established. **Amen.**

## CONFESSION

I declare that greater is he that is in me than he that is in the world. The greater one lives on the inside of me.

## Breakthrough Declaration 27

*Whenever I am afraid, I will trust in You.*

*Psalm 56:3*

---

**H**eavenly Father, I pray that this year you will help me to be still and to know that you are God. I declare by the power of the Holy Spirit that this year I will be still and see the victory of the power of the blood of Jesus over my life. I declare that when the storms and trials arise over my life this year that I will be still. When the enemy brings crisis, pain and torment over my life this year, I declare that I will be still and know that you are God over all the forces of darkness. I declare that I will find rest in Christ alone for He alone is the help and strength of my life. I declare order where there is disorder. I declare joy where there is sadness. I declare fruitfulness where there is barrenness. I proclaim peace where there is turmoil. I decree God's perfect will into my life, family, church and nation. In the day of God's visitation, He will cause kings to come to the brightness of my rising. This is my season for miracles, signs and wonders. **Amen.**

## CONFESSION

I shall not be moved from my place of victory. I will remain rooted and grounded in my position of victory in Christ. No matter the situation which comes my way I will be still and know that you are God.

## Breakthrough Declaration 28

*Finally, my brethren, be strong in the Lord and in the power of His might. Put on the whole armor of God, that you may be able to stand against the wiles of the devil.*

*Ephesians 6:10-11*

---

**H**eavenly **Father**, I declare that this year I will be strong in the Lord and in the power of his might. I put on the full armor of God so that I can stand against the devils schemes. I stand firm in the power of God and in the power of his might. I stand firm with the belt of truth buckled around my waist, with the breastplate of righteousness in place, and with my feet fitted with the readiness that comes from the gospel of peace. I take up the shield of faith, with which I can extinguish all the flaming arrows of the evil one. I take the helmet of salvation and the sword of the Spirit, which is the word of God. I pray in the Spirit on all occasions with all kinds of prayers and requests. With this in mind, I am alert and always keep on praying for all the Lord's people. **Amen.**

### CONFESSION

As a soldier of Christ, I declare that I am clothed and ready for battle. I am clothed with the full armor of God. I am clothed with the weapons of warfare. I am clothed with the garments of holiness and righteousness. I am clothed with the victory of Christ. I am matching on to greater victory this year. The cross before me and the world behind me.

## Breakthrough Declaration 29

*But Jesus looked at them and said to them, "With men this is impossible, but with God all things are possible."*
*Matthew 19:26*

---

**H**eavenly Father, thank You that I serve the God of the impossible. Thank You that all things are possible with You. I declare that what is impossible with man is possible only with the living God. I serve a big God who can do awesome things . I serve the God who is able to do all things. Father, I place my complete trust and confidence in you to do great and mighty things in my life this year. I will rest in your power and divine ability to make your power known to my enemies this year. The Lord will cause my enemies who rise against me to be defeated before my face. They shall come out against me one way and flee before me seven ways. They may come against me with intimidating weapons but every plan devised in hell shall not prosper in the name of Jesus. **Amen.**

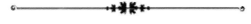

### CONFESSION

I declare that my God is an awesome God. He reigns with power, authority and is clothed with majesty. He holds the world in his hands and He can do all things. I look to him alone for he is my source, strength and refuge in this world of difficulty.

## Breakthrough Declaration 30

*Wait on the Lord; Be of good courage, and He shall strengthen your heart; Wait, I say, on the Lord!*

*Psalm 27:14*

---

**H**eavenly Father, I declare that this year, I will wait on the Lord. I will be strong and take heart. For you oh Lord are my strength and my shield. In you I take refuge against the storms and calamities which life might try to bring against me this year. Help me to at all times wait upon you and to be confident in your assurance to help me in my time of need for you have promised that you will never leave me nor forsake me. I decree and declare that with God's mighty hand, I overcome every giant and I experience victory in all areas of my life. I decree and declare that the heavens are opened unto me. I am experiencing a new season and I make a declaration that I am bigger, better and greater in the name of Jesus. **Amen.**

## CONFESSION

I declare that I will wait upon the Lord this year. He alone is my rock of refuge against the storms of life. I will not be moved for I will stand firm upon the solid Rock of Christ my Saviour. I decree and declare that the Lord will drive away every obstacle, mountain and impediment that stands in the way of my breakthrough in the name of Jesus.

## Breakthrough Declaration 31

*Trust in the LORD with all your heart,*
*and lean not on your own understanding;*
*In all your ways acknowledge Him, and*
*He shall direct your paths.*

*Proverbs 3:5-6*

---

**H**eavenly Father, I declare that I will trust in the Lord at all times. I will lean not unto my own understanding but in all of my ways I will acknowledge You for You shall direct my paths. I declare that this year I will trust in the Lord fully. I will delight in His ways for His plans for my life are the best. I thank you for complete direction and guidance in all areas of my life and destiny. I decree and declare that I step into this year full of confidence knowing that I am more than a conqueror. I am destined to walk in victory. I rejoice in my salvation and in the name of my God I raise a victory banner. **Amen.**

### CONFESSION

My trust is in the Lord. My confidence is in the Lord. My hope is in the Lord. My understanding is from the Lord. My direction is from the Lord. My guidance for living is from the Lord. My delight is in the Lord.

## Breakthrough Declaration 32

*I will go before you and make the crooked places straight; I will break in pieces the gates of bronze and cut the bars of iron. I will give you the treasures of darkness and hidden riches of secret places, that you may know that I, the Lord, Who call you by your name, am the God of Israel.*

*Isaiah 45:2-3*

---

**H**eavenly Father, thank you for going before me this year and making the crooked places straight. Thank you for breaking in pieces the gates of bronze and cutting the bars of iron. I receive the treasures of darkness and the hidden riches of secret places. I declare that the wealth of the unjust, the wicked and the unrighteous man is rightfully mine in the Name of Jesus. I declare that this year no assignment of the enemy can hinder or delay my financial miracle in the mighty Name of Jesus. I declare that You are the great and mighty God of Israel and I declare that this year you will make yourself known to the enemies of my breakthrough as the great I AM. **Amen.**

### CONFESSION

I declare that this is my year of accelerated financial breakthrough. This is my year of financial favor, blessings and investments. As a child of God I claim my inheritance which is mine through Jesus Christ.

## Breakthrough Declaration 33

*And you shall remember the Lord your God, for it is He who gives you power to get wealth, that He may establish His covenant which He swore to your fathers, as it is this day.*

*Deuteronomy 8:18*

Heavenly Father, help me to remember You today and always as the God who gives power to get wealth. This is your covenant promise to me, my children and their generation. I declare that I am walking in the blessings of Abraham. Help me to walk in obedience and faithfulness to your word and commands so that I can always enjoy your bountiful blessings. I decree and declare a double portion of blessing for my trouble. Double promotion, double increase, double wealth transfer, double healing for every tear I have cried, for every hurt and pain inflicted in the past, for every satanic trap set up for me, my family and my destiny. May God double my cup of blessings and cause it to overflow in the presence of my enemies. **Amen.**

### CONFESSION

The blessings of multiplied wealth and favor are mine in Christ. I declare that It is God who shall cause me to prosper in the presence of my enemies this year.

## Breakthrough Declaration 34

*If you are willing and obedient, you shall eat the good of the land.*

*Isaiah 1:19*

**H**eavenly Father, I declare that as I walk in obedience to your word I shall eat from the good of the land. I bind every demon and hindering spirit which is standing as a stumbling block to my financial breakthrough this year in the mighty name of Jesus Christ. I release angels with flaming swords of fire to push back and to destroy the devourer seeking to keep my life in bondage to poverty, debt and lack in the name of Jesus. I decree and declare that God is turning my darkness into light, my days of mourning into days of rejoicing. He is turning things around and this year I will expect God to do something new and unexpected in my life. **Amen.**

## CONFESSION

I declare that this year I will eat of the good of the land. I declare that I will drink from the well of my enemies and I will enjoy the fat of my blessings. I declare that God will display His power and glory upon my life for all men to see. They will see me rising but they will not be able to stop me in the name of Jesus.

## Breakthrough Declaration 35

*And my God shall supply all your need according to His riches in glory by Christ Jesus.*

*Philippians 4:19*

---

**H**eavenly Father, thank You that this year you have promised to supply all my needs according to your riches in glory through Christ Jesus. I look to you as my source, supplier, rewarder and provider. I thank you that I am rich in Christ Jesus. Thank you that you became poor so that I can be rich. I pray that you be magnified in every area of my life spiritually, financially and emotionally. Thank you for the provision of all my needs. I make a prophetic decree that I am stepping into a larger place. I am expanding to the right and to the left. The Lord is causing me to increase in every area of my life. He has enlarged my steps so that my feet do not slip. **Amen.**

## CONFESSION

I declare that all my needs are met. I will not worry, I will not doubt, I will not be afraid because my God has already promised that He will meet all my needs. My mind is at rest and I keep my mind stayed on Christ Jesus who is my Jehovah Jireh.

## Breakthrough Declaration 36

*But seek first the kingdom of God and His righteousness, and all these things shall be added to you. Therefore do not worry about tomorrow, for tomorrow will worry about its own things. Sufficient for the day is its own trouble.*

*Matthew 6:33-34*

---

**H**eavenly Father, I pray that this year You will help me to seek first the kingdom of God and your righteousness. I thank You that as I seek first Your kingdom which is my main priority, you have promised that all things which are according to Your will shall be added to me. I declare that this year I will not worry about tomorrow for You are the God who has promised to supply all of my needs. I decree and declare according to Psalm 68:19 "Blessed be the Lord, Who daily loads us with benefits, the God of our salvation!" **Amen.**

## CONFESSION

I make a bold confession that this year I will not worry about anything. I declare that my mind, spirit, soul and body is at rest confidently trusting in the Lord. As I look towards this year I will remember to trust and be confident in my God always.

## Breakthrough Declaration 37

*I have been young, and now am old; yet I have not seen the righteous forsaken, nor his descendants begging bread.*

**Psalm 37:25**

Heavenly Father, thank You that You have promised to never leave us nor forsake us. I thank You that this year I, my children nor family will be forsaken. I thank You that my descendants will not beg for bread. I veto and cancel every plan of the enemy to cause me financial ruin or cause us to become beggars. Thank You for Your trust and assurance that the righteous will never be moved. I stand on Your word and declare that this year I shall not be moved in the name of Jesus. I break every curse or covenant of poverty in my generation in the mighty name of Jesus. Thank you Lord for keeping me safe from the deadly pestilence, the snare of the fowler, satanic fiery darts of the enemy, pits, traps, dungeons, and though an army should surround me, God will deliver me today. **Amen.**

### CONFESSION

I declare that I am the righteousness of God in Christ Jesus. I declare that I will never be forsaken. My children or my family will never be forsaken in the name of Jesus. I decree and declare that we will not beg for bread because Christ died so that I will be rich and not poor.

## Breakthrough Declaration 38

*The blessing of the Lord makes one rich,*
*and He adds no sorrow with it.*
                                    **Proverbs 10:22**

---

**H**eavenly Father, thank You that the blessing of the Lord which makes one rich is evident upon my life. I declare that this year I will seek the blessing of the Lord and nothing else. I annihilate every demonic plan of the devil to bring sorrow into my life this year in the name of Jesus. I declare that as I walk in the blessing of the Lord riches, favor, promotion, health, strength, peace and long life are being added unto me in the Name of Jesus. I make a bold declaration that I will rest, relax and bask in the blessing of the Lord with the peace which comes from Him alone. I reject every other worldly thing which men are seeking to find peace in and I embrace the true peace which comes from Christ alone. **Amen.**

## CONFESSION

I am walking in the blessing of the Lord. I am walking in peace, favor, happiness, prosperity and long life all the days of my life. I destroy the plans of the enemy to bring sorrow, discord and confusion into my life this year. I declare that I will enjoy the blessings of the Lord in peace.

## Breakthrough Declaration 39

*May the Lord give you increase more and more, you and your children.*

*Psalm 115:14*

---

**H**eavenly Father, I declare this year you will cause me and my children to increase more and more. I prophetically declare that the increase of the Lord is upon my life, my family and my children. I declare that the anointing for increase and wealth is upon my household in the name of Jesus. I declare that this year we will increase in wealth, stature, favor and prominence with God and men all the days of our lives in the mighty name of Jesus Christ. I declare great doors are opened to me and I boldly take possession of the gates of my enemies. This is my season and no one can stop my breakthroughs. This is my prophetic season and I decree and declare them upon my life. This is my season of exploits. I am blessed with abundant increase in power , wisdom, wealth, riches and with a life time of God's limitless favor. **Amen.**

### CONFESSION

The blessings of the Lord bring increase. I confess that the blessings of the Lord are upon my children. I declare that they are blessed and not cursed. I declare that the blessings of the Lord will follow them all the days of their lives and they will be blessed.

## Breakthrough Declaration 40

*The young lions lack and suffer hunger; but those who seek the Lord shall not lack any good thing.*

*Psalm 34:10*

Heavenly Father, thank you that those who seek the Lord shall not lack any good thing. I declare that as I seek the Lord my family and I shall not lack any good thing this year in the name of Jesus. I declare that I and my family will not suffer from hunger or financial famine this year in the name of Jesus. I break every demonic curse of the enemy which would cause us to miss out on the blessings of the Lord. Father, let every breakthrough, potential, elevation, growth, advancement, that is being held captive by the enemy be released now in the mighty name of Jesus Christ of Nazareth. Let every captivity of the enemy be turned around now in the mighty name of Jesus Christ of Nazareth. **Amen.**

### CONFESSION

I declare that my desire is to seek first the Lord. As I seek the Lord no good thing shall be withheld from me. This is my covenant promise in Christ therefore I claim it through faith.

## Breakthrough Declaration 41

*The earth is the Lord's, and all its fullness,*
*the world and those who dwell therein.*
*Psalm 24:1*

**H**eavenly Father, I declare that you are the God of heaven and earth. The great and mighty God who created and rules over all things. I declare that the earth and everything in it belongs to you. I thank you that you have given to us all things to enjoy as your children. I declare that this is your covenant promise to us therefore by faith I declare that I am blessed with all things. Father, I decree and declare that a new day and a new season has come into my life. Thank you Lord for the oil of gladness which surrounds my life. Thank You for the joy of the Lord which is my strength. Thank You for making me the head always and causing me to walk in victory. **Amen.**

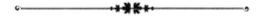

## CONFESSION

I declare that all things belong to my God. As a child of God I claim my inheritance in Christ as a rightful heir of all that belongs to me in this earth. I declare that I am blessed with silver, gold, precious stones, houses, lands, livestock , vehicles and everything else in this world which the Lord has given to me.

## Breakthrough Declaration 42

*Beloved, I pray that you may prosper in all things and be in health, just as your soul prospers.*

*3 John 1:2*

---

**H**eavenly Father, thank you that it is Your desire that I prosper and be in health just as my soul prospers. Thank you Lord that I am blessed spiritually, financially, emotionally and the blessings of the Lord radiates in all areas of my life. I declare that this year prosperity in wealth, body, soul and spirit is mine. I declare that I have good health and I cancel every assignment of sickness and disease in my body in the mighty name of Jesus Christ. I receive the blessings of God's perfect gift. I will come into the completion and into the fullness of God's perfect will for my life and destiny. The lines will fall in pleasant places for me. There shall be no delays. There shall be no stagnation. My gift will make room for me and bring me before great men. I will prosper in all things. **Amen.**

### CONFESSION

I declare that I prosper in every single area of life. My prosperity is not just limited to wealth but health and wholeness. Thank you for taking care of my holistic well-being.

## Breakthrough Declaration 43

*By humility and the fear of the Lord are riches and honor and life.*

*Proverbs 22:4*

---

**H**eavenly Father, I pray that this year You would help me to walk in humility and the fear of the Lord. I pray that as I walk in these virtues with a sincere heart that I would enjoy the blessings of riches, honor and life. I bind and rebuke every ungodly, fleshly and carnal desires of the flesh which wars against my spirit man in the name of Jesus. I break and destroy the strongholds of pride, arrogance, and every other demonic spirit which would hinder me from receiving the blessings of the Lord. I repent of every evil way and I ask for Your forgiveness for anything in my life which stands as a barrier to the blessings of the Lord in my life. **Amen.**

## CONFESSION

I declare that I am walking in the spirit of humility and the fear of the Lord. I declare that riches, honor and life are mine.

## Breakthrough Declaration 44

*Thus says the Lord, your Redeemer, The Holy One of Israel: "I am the Lord your God, Who teaches you to profit, Who leads you by the way you should go.*

*Isaiah 48:17*

**H**eavenly Father, thank You that you are the Lord, my Redeemer, The Holy One of Israel. I declare that You are the God who teaches me to profit. I command every spirit of lack operating in my life to be nullified in the name of Jesus. I command the gates of my prosperity and financial breakthrough to be opened in the name of Jesus. I pray that every seed which has been sown would begin to bear good fruit and yield a harvest in the Name of Jesus. I command the devour assigned to hinder my harvest to be paralyzed in the mighty name of Jesus Christ. I pray Father that you would lead me in the way I should go this year. Open my eyes that I might see opportunities for wealth generation and increase in the Name of Jesus. **Amen.**

## CONFESSION

I declare that it is the will and desire of God for me to prosper this year. I stand on the word of God and declare that I will prosper and walk in my covenant blessings.

## Breakthrough Declaration 45

*And I will make your descendants multiply as the stars of heaven; I will give to your descendants all these lands; and in your seed all the nations of the earth shall be blessed; because Abraham obeyed My voice and kept My charge, My commandments, My statutes, and My laws.*

*Genesis 26:4-5*

---

**H**eavenly Father, thank You that you will make my descendants multiply as the stars of heaven. I declare that this year I am possessing all that is rightfully mine in the name of Jesus. I thank you Lord that through my seed, all nations of the earth shall be blessed in the Name of Jesus. I declare that my seed is anointed for mighty exploits in the earth. **Amen.**

## CONFESSION

I declare that my children and their generation shall be great in the earth. I declare that they are anointed and blessed for signs and wonders in their generation. I annihilate and exterminate every plan of the enemy to destroy and sabotage the purpose, calling and destiny of God's perfect plan for my generation in this earth.

## Breakthrough Declaration 46

*For every beast of the forest is Mine, and the cattle on a thousand hills.*

**Psalm 50:10**

---

**H**eavenly **Father,** thank You that everything in this earth belongs to You. You are Jehovah Elohim. You are the Creator of all things and I thank you that You have given to me dominion over everything which belongs to you. I declare that I am blessed to be a blessing to all men. I declare that all the days of my life men shall call me blessed in the Name of Jesus. I claim and receive all my blessings in Jesus' mighty and matchless name. This is my season of abundance and overflow. I am rising up from the ashes to take my rightful place in Christ Jesus, Hallelujah! I am blessed, my family is blessed, everything and everyone connected to me is blessed. I serve a miracle-working, destiny-changing God. Thank you Lord for elevation and greater works. **Amen.**

### CONFESSION

I declare that I am blessed with great riches and treasures of this earth. My Father owns everything and I declare that I am an heir to his inheritance. I declare that I shall enjoy all that God has given to me.

## Breakthrough Declaration 47

*Let them shout for joy and be glad, Who favor my righteous cause; and let them say continually, "Let the Lord be magnified, who has pleasure in the prosperity of His servant."*

*Psalm 35:27*

---

**H**eavenly Father, I declare that You are magnified in every area of my life. I release a shout of joy and gladness and prophesy over my life this year that You are magnified Oh Lord Almighty! I thank You that You delight in my prosperity. I declare that because the Lord delights in my prosperity, I am blessed and not cursed. I am the head and not the tail. I am a lender and not a borrower in the Name of Jesus. I decree and declare that I am entering into a new season of miracles and in this year God will show me favor. He will open impossible doors, break the rocks of reproach and pour upon me a blessing of a thousand times more. I will increase on every side. I shall do greater works because Jehovah will magnify me in the sight of men. This is my season to shine! **Amen.**

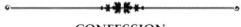

### CONFESSION

Be magnified Oh Lord for You are highly exalted over my life, finances, children, family, business, career and ministry this year. I declare that there is no one like You. Thank You for taking pleasure and delight in seeing me prosper.

## Breakthrough Declaration 48

*They are abundantly satisfied with the fullness of Your house, and You give them drink from the river of Your pleasures. For with You is the fountain of life; in Your light we see light.*

*Psalm 36:8-9*

---

**H**eavenly Father, I declare that this year I will be abundantly satisfied with the fullness of your house. I declare that I will drink from the river of Your pleasures. I declare that You are a fountain of life and in Your light we see light. I declare that you are the fountain of my life. I thank you that all good things comes from You and I delight in You. I decree and declare that I receive favor, divine access, increase, establishment and expansion in every area of my life. I will be recognized, lifted up and celebrated. The Lord will multiply me and increase me abundantly. He will make me a thousand times wiser, glorious, mightier, bigger, better and greater! **Amen.**

## CONFESSION

I declare that You are the source of my wealth. You are the fountain of my life. I delight myself in you. I am satisfied with the good things which comes from you.

## Breakthrough Declaration 49

*You crown the year with Your goodness,*
*and Your paths drip with abundance.*
*Psalm 65:11*

---

**H**eavenly **Father,** thank You for crowning my year with Your goodness. I declare that my paths drip with abundance. Thank You for going before me and crowning my year with Your bounty. Thank You that I am walking in the overflow of your supernatural blessings. I declare that my steps shall be ordered by the Lord this year. Supernatural increase and divine provision shall be my portion this year in the name of Jesus. I decree and declare that the heavens are opened unto me by faith. I receive the answer to every prayer I have uttered. I step into the acceptable year of the Lord in full confidence, knowing that God will do exceedingly, abundantly above all that I ask or think. I walk in supernatural favour and the glory of the Lord will be seen upon me. **Amen.**

## CONFESSION

My year is crowned with goodness. My life is overflowing with Your abundance. All that I have is blessed. There shall be no lack. The windows of heaven are opened and I divinely receive supernatural blessings.

## Breakthrough Declaration 50

*I traverse the way of righteousness,*
*In the midst of the paths of justice,*
*that I may cause those who love me*
*to inherit wealth, that I may fill their*
*treasuries.*

*Proverbs 8:20-21*

---

Heavenly Father, thank You that You delight when we traverse in the way of righteousness and the paths of justice. Help me to delight myself in the wisdom of the Lord that You may cause me to inherit wealth and true riches, because of my great love for You that you may fill my treasuries. I declare that I am a person of righteousness, integrity and moral standing. Help me Father to never walk in the way of the ungodly that your blessings may evade me. I declare that every evil activity in my life, my children's life, my job, business and my family shall cease by the precious blood of Jesus Christ. I declare that the blood speaks more than the blood of Abel. Henceforth I stand on the solid rock Jesus Christ to declare safety in my home and also declare that I am preserved from the attacks of the enemy in the mighty Name of Jesus Christ. **Amen.**

### CONFESSION

I declare that I walk in righteousness and the way of justice. I abhor any evil way and repent from any wickedness which would cause me to miss out on the blessings of the Lord.

## Breakthrough Declaration 51

*So let each one give as he purposes in his heart, not grudgingly or of necessity; for God loves a cheerful giver. And God is able to make all grace abound toward you, that you, always having all sufficiency in all things, may have an abundance for every good work. As it is written: "He has dispersed abroad, He has given to the poor; His righteousness endures forever."*

*2 Corinthians 9:7-9*

---

**H**eavenly Father, I declare that I am a cheerful giver of my tithes and offerings. I repent of withholding anything which rightfully belongs to You. Thank You for making all grace abound towards me so that I always having all sufficiency in all things may have an abundance for every good work. I declare that You are the God who takes care of the poor and I thank you that Your righteousness endures forever. **Amen.**

## CONFESSION

I give back to the Lord with a glad, cheerful and open heart from the resources which he has blessed me with. I repent if I have ever given grudgingly or under compulsion. Thank You for making all grace abound towards me this year as I continue to give with a free, open and willing heart of love and sacrifice.

## Breakthrough Declaration 52

*Now may He who supplies seed to the sower, and bread for food, supply and multiply the seed you have sown and increase the fruits of your righteousness.*

*2 Corinthians 9:10*

Heavenly Father, thank You that You are the God who supplies seed to the sower and bread for food. I pray that this year You will supply and multiply the seeds I have sown in your kingdom and that you would increase the fruits of my righteousness. I give thanks and praise to you for doing all this and so much more for me and my family this year. **Amen.**

## CONFESSION

I declare that very seed sown into the kingdom of God shall yield its harvest this year. I declare that my seed shall multiply and I will increase in righteousness. There shall be no lack or scarcity for God shall honor my giving. Where there is seed time there must be a harvest.

## Breakthrough Declaration 53

*Bring all the tithes into the storehouse, That there may be food in My house, and try Me now in this," Says the Lord of hosts," If I will not open for you the windows of heaven and pour out for you such blessing   that there   will not be room enough to receive it.*

*Malachi 3:10*

---

**H**eavenly Father, I repent and ask for Your forgiveness if at any time I have robbed You and Your kingdom of the tithes and offerings which rightfully belong to you. I pray that the curse over my life and finances would be broken in the name of Jesus. As I open my heart to give and to sow into Your kingdom I thank You for opening the windows of heaven and pouring out a blessing that there will not be room enough to receive. I declare that this year the windows of heaven are opened over my children, finances, businesses and every area which I am facing a financial famine. I declare the rain of Your abundance is flowing over my life right now in the name of Jesus. **Amen.**

### CONFESSION

As I give of my tithes and offerings I am believing God for a season of open heavens over my life this year. I declare that there shall be manifestations of signs, wonders and supernatural miracles in my finances. I declare that bills, debts and mortgages are paid in full.

## Breakthrough Declaration 54

*And I will rebuke the devourer for your sakes, So that he will not destroy the fruit of your ground, Nor shall the vine fail to bear fruit for you in the field," Says the Lord of hosts.*

*Malachi 3:11*

---

**H**eavenly **Father,** thank You for rebuking the devourer for my sake so that he will not destroy the fruit of my ground. I declare that this year the vine shall not fail to bear fruit for me in my field. I declare that the seed which I have sown into the kingdom of God shall not fail to bring a harvest or to multiply in the Name of Jesus. I break every curse of bankruptcy, financial famine and lack over my finances this year in the mighty name of Jesus Christ. I declare that I will eat and be satisfied in the Name of Jesus. **Amen.**

## CONFESSION

I declare that every curse of financial failure is broken over my life. I break the curse of poverty, debts, unpaid bills and struggling to make ends meet. I prophetically declare that the devourer is rebuked and the heavens are opened over my life this year. I will receive the rain of the Lord blessings. Send your rain oh Lord.

## Breakthrough Declaration 55

*And all nations will call you blessed, For you will be a delightful land," Says the Lord of hosts.*

*Malachi 3:12*

**H**eavenly Father ,I declare that when I give faithfully of my tithes and offerings all nations shall call me blessed. I declare that I will be a delightful land. Thank You that I am blessed and not cursed. I declare that my children shall rise up and call me blessed in the Name of Jesus. I declare that strangers shall be a blessing to me and the work of my hands shall reap a plentiful harvest in the Name of Jesus. I decree and declare that this is my year of abundance, supernatural breakthrough and favour. I declare the glory of God is upon me and my family in Jesus mighty name. God will surprise me with His goodness this year that will dumbfound everyone around me. **Amen.**

### CONFESSION

I declare that I am blessed and not cursed. My handiwork is blessed and prosperous. Nations shall call me blessed. I will be a delightful land. The work of my hands shall be blessed.

## Breakthrough Declaration 56

*Give, and it will be given to you: good measure, pressed down, shaken together, and running over will be put into your bosom. For with the same measure that you use, it will be measured back to you."*

*Luke 6:38*

---

Heavenly Father, I declare that I am a cheerful giver. I give with purpose and expectation that your will be done in every area of my life. Help me to never become selfish or hold back in giving what is rightfully Yours. I thank You that all things belong to You and I am only a steward of all the good things which you have blessed me with in my life. The Lord has filled my mouth with good things. There is an overflow of abundance. I am the Lord Your God, who brought you out of the land of Egypt; open your mouth wide, and I will fill it. (Ps 81:10). In this season, I will wrestle in prayer and prevail. The Lord will cause me to triumph over my fears. I will win over the enemy. Mountains will move before me and every resistance will crumble. The Lord will lift me from the valley and set me upon my high mountain. **Amen.**

### CONFESSION

As I sow sparingly, I declare that I will reap sparingly. As I sow bountifully, I declare that I will reap bountifully this year in the name of Jesus.

## Breakthrough Declaration 57

*And my God shall supply all your need according to His riches in glory by Christ Jesus.*

*Philippians 4:19*

---

**H**eavenly Father, thank You for supplying all of my needs according to Your riches in glory by Christ Jesus. I declare that all my needs are met this year in the Name of Jesus. Thank You for being the great supplier of everything that I need. Thank You Lord that I can come before you knowing that you will respond to every prayer prayed according to your divine will and purpose for my life. I declare that in Christ, I possess great riches of wealth, prosperity, health, peace, salvation, grace and mercy. Thank You for making those great riches in glory available to me. May the Lord fill my mouth with good things. May He fill my empty barrels to the overflow. Abundance of peace, love, wisdom, and blessings are coming my way. I receive my blessing, favour, marriage, grace, prosperity and the Lord is filling my mouth and empty barrels with abundant blessings in Jesus Name. **Amen.**

### CONFESSION

I possess the great riches in glory by Christ Jesus. All things are mine. I lay hold of it to the honor and glory of his blessed name.

## Breakthrough Declaration 58

*The Lord is my shepherd; I shall not want. He makes me to lie down in green pastures; He leads me beside the still waters. He restores my soul; He leads me in the paths of righteousness For His name's sake.*

*Psalm 23:1-4*

---

**H**eavenly Father, thank You for being my Shepherd. You are Jehovah Roi the Good Shepherd. Thank you for meeting my every basic need of food, shelter and clothing. Thank you Lord for causing me to lie down in green pastures. Thank you for leading me beside the still waters. Thank you for restoring my soul and leading me in the paths of righteousness for your name's sake. I decree and declare that in this season, the Lord will make me bigger, better and greater. I will spread my wings as the eagle and I will rise to your high places. I receive the blessing of new wells. In this season, the Lord will open to me the treasures of the deep. I will dig and find water. The Lord will make room for me. **Amen.**

### CONFESSION

I declare that this year the Lord will be my Shepherd. Thank You for Your provision, rest, guidance and comfort in every area of my life.

## Breakthrough Declaration 59

*And Abraham called the name of the place, The-LORD-Will-Provide; as it is said to this day, "In the Mount of the LORD it shall be provided."*

*Genesis 22:14*

---

**H**eavenly Father, I declare that You are my Jehovah Jireh the Lord who provides my every need. Thank You for providing and continuing to provide for me and my family this year. I declare that You are my El Shaddai, the God who is more than enough. Thank You for being my source. I declare that my hope, trust and confidence is in You alone. I declare that there shall be no scarcity and lack in my life this year in the Name of Jesus. I decree in the name of Jesus that I will accomplish my assignment. I decree and declare the full manifestation of the purposes of God in my life. I declare in this season that doors are opening, gateways opening, highways opening, revelation, success, breakthrough and petitions in the courts of heaven granted. I declare injustices against my life are overruled in the name of Jesus. **Amen.**

## CONFESSION

The Lord is the source of all that I possess. Everything that I have belongs to Him. He is my provider. Because He lives I can face tomorrow without worry knowing He will take care of me.

## Breakthrough Declaration 60

*He shall be like a tree planted by the rivers of water, That brings forth its fruit in its season, Whose leaf also shall not wither; And whatever he does shall prosper.*

*Psalm 1:3*

---

**H**eavenly **Father,** because I delight and meditate greatly in You and Your commandments, I declare that I shall be like a tree planted by the rivers of water that brings forth fruit in its season. I declare that my leaf shall not wither and whatever I do shall prosper in the Name of Jesus. I declare that as I meditate day and night in the word of the living God my life shall be a sweet success. Everything that I do shall be blessed because I trust in the Lord. I declare the showers of the Lords blessings are raining over my life right now in the name of Jesus. **Amen.**

### CONFESSION

I am like a tree planted by the rivers of water that brings forth its fruit in its season. My life does not wither, become dull, dry or experience famine. Whatever I do this year shall prosper.

## Breakthrough Declaration 61

*Peace be within your walls, prosperity within your palaces."*

**Psalm 122:7**

---

**H**eavenly Father, thank You that this year I will enjoy the peace of the Lord. I declare peace and prosperity shall be in my house. I cancel every assignment of the enemy to bring disruption, chaos and confusion in my house in the name of Jesus. Thank you Lord for Your great peace and prosperity. I declare peace within my borders in the Name of Jesus. The peace of God which surpasses all understanding guards my heart and mind. In times of trouble, His peace covers me. I declare the God of peace will crush satan under my feet. Every work of the enemy shall come to nothing. No weapon designed against me shall prosper. **Amen.**

## CONFESSION

I declare peace in every area of my life. I declare that the peace of the Lord reigns supreme in my life. I declare prosperity shall be in my house. There shall not be any place for lack.

## Breakthrough Declaration 62

*That our barns may be full, Supplying all kinds of produce; That our sheep may bring forth thousands And ten thousands in our fields; That our oxen may be well laden; That there be no breaking in or going out; That there be no outcry in our streets.*

*Psalm 144:13-14*

---

**H**eavenly Father, I declare Your blessings in every area of my life. I declare that my barn is full and supplying all kinds of produce. I declare that my sheep is bringing forth thousands and ten thousands in my field. I declare that my oxen is well laden and there is no breaking in or going out. I declare that there is no outcry in the streets in the name of Jesus. Thank You for Your promises of prosperity and blessings to Your children. I pray that my barns be filled with plenty and presses burst with new wine in the name of Jesus. **Amen.**

## CONFESSION

I declare my cupboard is full of groceries, my land is blessed with fruits, vegetables and all manner of provision. I declare my cattle, sheep and goat is blessed and there is no sound of violence in the streets this year.

## Breakthrough Declaration 63

*So I will restore to you the years that the swarming locust has eaten, The crawling locust, The consuming locust, and the chewing locust, My great army which I sent among you.*

*Joel 2:25*

---

**H**eavenly Father, thank you that You are the Mighty Restorer. I pray that Lord You will restore to me the years that the enemy came in and stole and devoured my blessings, health, family, marriage, peace and finances in the Name of Jesus. I take back everything which the enemy has stolen from me this year in the Name of Jesus. **Amen.**

## CONFESSION

I declare that I am taking back everything which the enemy has stolen from me. I command the strongman to release what rightfully belongs to me. I release fire into the camp of the enemy and I pursue, overtake and recover all that I have lost over the years.

## Breakthrough Declaration 64

*The angel of the Lord encamps around those who fear him, and he delivers them.*

*Psalm 34:7*

---

**H**eavenly Father, thank You that the angels of the Lord are watching over me and my family this year. I declare that we are surrounded with armies of angels who stand guard over us night and day because we walk in the fear of the Lord. Thank You Lord for deliverance from the plots, tactics, plans and conspiracies of the enemy concerning my life this year in the name of Jesus. I declare and decree that this is my year of divine miracle of signs and wonders. I step into supernatural favor and protection from the evil ways of wicked enemies. By faith I nullify every bad declaration and word curses in my life and forever will I live under an opened heaven. **Amen.**

### CONFESSION

The angels of the Lord are watching over me and my family. I am not afraid because the Lord of Host is with me. Angels are around my children, my house, my family, vehicles and everything which I possess. Deliverance comes from the Lord.

## Breakthrough Declaration 65

*You will keep in perfect peace those whose minds are steadfast, because they trust in You.*

*Isaiah 26:3*

---

**H**eavenly Father, thank You for the perfect peace which comes from You alone. I declare that I have peace this year because my mind is steadfast trusting in the Lord. I cancel every plan of the enemy to cause my mind to be disturbed with fear, bad news and confusion in the Name of Jesus. Because I trust in the Lord, I shall not be moved from my position of victory. I declare that my life is secured in Christ. My family, children, siblings, loved ones are all secured in Christ Jesus. I decree and declare that our lives are impenetrable to the satanic devices of the enemy seeking to destabilize our peace in Christ. May our minds remain steadfast in You as we continue to place our trust and confidence in You. **Amen.**

## CONFESSION

I have perfect peace which comes from trusting in Christ alone. I will trust in no other for in him I am steadfast, unmovable and unshakable.

## Breakthrough Declaration 66

*Those who sow with tears will reap with songs of joy.*

Psalm 126:5

---

**H**eavenly Father, I declare that though I sow with tears I will reap with songs of joy. I declare that the joy of the Lord will be my strength this year. I declare that this year I will sing songs of joy and not sorrow in the Name of Jesus. I declare that for every tear which I have cried, laughter shall be my portion this year in the Name of Jesus. I declare the power of expansion, the force of influence, the breaking down of demonic strongholds, enemies under my feet, the blessing of dominion, the blessing of elevation, the blessing of possession is overtaking my life. I declare comfort in the place of mourning. I declare I will songs of victory and not defeat in the Name of Jesus. **Amen.**

### CONFESSION

Laughter and joy shall be my portion this year. Every enemy seeking to bring sorrow and sadness in my life this year shall be disgraced.

## Breakthrough Declaration 67

*He put a new song in my mouth, a hymn of praise to our God. Many will see and fear the Lord and put their trust in him.*

*Psalm 40:3*

**H**eavenly Father, I declare that this year You shall put a new song in my mouth, a hymn of praise to our God. I declare that this year I will sing only songs of victory and not defeat in the Name of Jesus. I declare that many will see the power of God at work in my life and will put their trust in Him. I will not hold back because the Greater One lives inside of me. Blessed is the Lord who enlarges me. I receive grace to conceive and to receive more. May the Lord make me a thousand times more than my fathers. The Lord will take me to my Rehoboth - my place of peace, a place of settlement and a place of enlargement. The Lord will make room for me and I shall be fruitful in the earth. **Amen.**

### CONFESSION

God has put a new song in my mouth. Praise is my weapon of victory against the enemy this year. Many will see and fear the Lord and put their trust in him.

## Breakthrough Declaration 68

*He restores my soul. He guides me in paths of righteousness for his name's sake.*

*Psalm 23:3*

---

**H**eavenly Father, thank You for restoring my soul this year. I declare that You are the God of total and complete restoration. Thank You for guiding me in the paths of righteousness for Your name's sake. I declare that I am healed from brokenness, rejection, hurt, anger, unforgiveness, bitterness jealousy, envy, resentment and every other form of bondage which I have allowed to control my life negatively. I repent and ask Your forgiveness if I have inadvertently hurt anyone and I ask You to redeem my life from destruction. I pray that this day would be a day of new beginnings and I receive your love, tender mercies and kindness which is new every morning. Thank You for loving me unconditionally and help me to reciprocate the same love that you have for me towards others. Be magnified in and through my life. **Amen.**

### CONFESSION

God is restoring my soul. Every broken and bruised area in my life is being healed and mended. I am free for whom the Son has set free is truly free indeed. God has liberated my life from the bondage of the enemy. Thank You Lord for such wonderful freedom that we have in Christ Jesus.

## Breakthrough Declaration 69

*So shall My word be that goes forth from My mouth; It shall not return to Me void, But it shall accomplish what I please, And it shall prosper in the thing for which I sent it.*

*Isaiah 55:11*

---

Heavenly Father, thank You that Your word which goes forth from Your mouth shall not return to You void. I declare the power of Your word is bringing transformation into my life and circumstances. Thank You that Your word shall accomplish what You please and it shall prosper in the thing for which You sent it. I decree and declare that Your word shall accomplish its divine purpose in my life this year in the Name of Jesus. I receive the blessing of divine mercy and grace. The Lord will be merciful to me. Instead of judgement, I will find mercy. In this season, the grace of the Lord will be multiplied over me. I declare grace for salvation, grace for uncommon favor, grace to overcome adversity, grace to overcome my weakness, grace to finish well, grace to be a blessing, grace to be a deliverer. **Amen.**

### CONFESSION

Thank you Lord for the power of Your word. I declare that your word is working powerfully in my life. Thank you for the divine power of Your word which brings prosperity in the midst of every situation of life.

## Breakthrough Declaration 70

*But know that the Lord has set apart for Himself him who is godly; The Lord will hear when I call to Him.*

*Psalm 4:3*

---

**H**eavenly Father, thank You for setting me apart for yourself. Help me to continue walking in righteousness and pursuing the way of godliness. Lord my prayer this year is that You would use me for Your honor and Your glory. Thank You Lord that You will hear when I call to You. Thank You that because I walk uprightly You will hear and answer my every prayer. I receive the declaration & proclaim I will arise & shine for my time has come because Christ has finished the work on the cross. **Amen.**

## CONFESSION

I am set apart to be used by God. I walk in holiness and righteousness. The Lord will hear me when I call unto Him.

## Breakthrough Declaration 71

*The Lord opens the eyes of the blind; The Lord raises those who are bowed down; the Lord loves the righteous.*

*Psalm 146:8*

---

**H**eavenly Father, Thank you for opening the eyes of the blind. Thank you for raising those who are bowed down. Thank you Lord for loving the righteous. I declare that this year you will open the eyes of all those who are blind spiritually and you will restore vision that we may see and experience Your truth. Thank you that You are able to lift us when we are bowed. **Amen.**

## CONFESSION

My eyes are open to receive spiritual truth. The Lord shall raise me up when I am bowed down. The Lord loves the righteous.

## Breakthrough Declaration 72

*The steps of a good man are ordered by the Lord, and He delights in his way. Though he fall, he shall not be utterly cast down; For the Lord upholds him with His hand.*
*Psalms 37:23-24*

---

**H**eavenly Father, I declare that this year the Lord will order my steps according to His word. Thank You Lord that the steps of a good man are ordered by the Lord, and he delights in his way. I declare that though I fall I shall not be utterly cast down, for the Lord upholds me with His hand. But the Lord my God will deliver my enemies over to me, throwing them into great confusion until they are destroyed. Deuteronomy 7:23. I walk in the supernatural favour and the glory of God I receive answers to every prayer uttered and I know God will perform miracles and wonders upon my life in Jesus' Name. **Amen.**

### CONFESSION

My steps are ordered by the Lord and God delights in my way. Don't rejoice over me when I fall for the Lord upholds me with his mighty hand.

## Breakthrough Declaration 73

*For the Lord will be your confidence, and will keep your foot from being caught.*

*Proverbs. 3:26*

---

**H**eavenly Father, I declare that this year You will be my confidence and You will keep my foot from being caught from the plots of wickedness. I declare that this year I will boast in the confidence of my God. I decree and declare that the plans of the wicked shall not prosper in my life this year because the Lord will be my confidence. I am victorious in Christ. For they intended evil against me; they devised a plot which they are not able to perform. God frustrates the devices of the crafty, so that their hands cannot carry out their plans. The Lord brings the counsel of the nations to nothing; He makes the plans of the peoples of no effect. - Psalm 21:11, 33:10; Job 5:12. Thank You Lord for keeping me safe from the secret counsels of the wicked and the insurrection of the workers of iniquity. **Amen.**

### CONFESSION

The Lord is my victory. He is my confidence. My assurance of victory comes from him alone. My foot will not be caught in the snare of the enemy this year.

## Breakthrough Declaration 74

*And the Lord shall help them and deliver them; He shall deliver them from the wicked, And save them, Because they trust in Him.*

*Psalm 37:40*

---

**H**eavenly **Father,** thank You that You will help me and deliver me from the wicked who are planning and conspiring against my life this year. Thank You for delivering me from the plans of the wicked and saving me because I trust in You. I declare that those who wage war against me will be ashamed because the Lord is my defense. The Lord is my strength, my shield and my helper. The Lord is my rock, my fortress, my deliverer and my buckler. Behold all those who are angered against me will surely be ashamed and confounded. The wicked shall perish, and the enemies of the Lord shall be as the fat of lambs. They shall be consumed in the Name of Jesus. I decree in the name of Jesus, by the blood of Jesus, that every weapon formed against me will not prosper. **Amen.**

### CONFESSION

I declare that the Lord shall help me. He is my deliverer. I am delivered from the conspiracy of the wicked. He will save me because I trust in Him.

## Breakthrough Declaration 75

*I am the Lord Your God, who brought you out of the land of Egypt; open your mouth wide, and I will fill it.*

*Psalm 81:10*

---

**H**eavenly Father, thank you for filling me and bringing seasons of restoration into my life. Thank You for deliverance from the bondage of Egypt. I declare that the chains and shackles of oppression and bondage are broken over my life this year in the Name of Jesus. Thank You for filling my life with Your blessings. I declare that everything I lost in the past shall be restored to me in the Name of Jesus. I declare that this is my season of restoration. I will never despise the days of small beginning because I know that in due season my God will surely reward me. God continues to give me strength. My beginnings may seem small and ordinary, yet extraordinary and prosperous will my future be. **Amen.**

## CONFESSION

I declare that bondage and oppression is broken over my life this year. God is restoring everything that was stolen from me and is filling my life with the goodness of His bounty.

## Breakthrough Declaration 76

*Call to Me, and I will answer you, and show you great and mighty things, which you do not know.*

*Jeremiah 33:3*

---

**H**eavenly Father, thank You that You have promised in your word if I call upon You, You will answer me and show me great and mighty things I do not know. Thank You that in the day of trouble You will hear my cry and deliver me from the conspiracy of the enemy. I declare the Lord is the help and strength of my life. I release a breakthrough atmosphere over my home, my ministry, family and command satanic barricades and blockages to be divinely removed in the name of Jesus Christ. I access the supernatural favour of God. God shall do exceedingly abundantly above all that my family and I have asked of Him in Jesus name. We enter into the acceptable season of God in full confidence. **Amen.**

### CONFESSION

I will call upon the Lord who is worthy of my praise and I will be saved from my enemies. When I call upon the Lord he will reveal great and mighty things to me.

## Breakthrough Declaration 77

*God is our refuge and strength, A very present help in trouble.*

*Psalm 46:1*

---

**H**eavenly Father, I declare that this year You shall be my refuge and my strength. You are a very present help in trouble. I declare according to Psalm 63:3-5, "Because Your loving kindness is better than life, My lips shall praise You. Thus I will bless You while I live; I will lift up my hands in Your name. My soul shall be satisfied as with marrow and fatness, and my mouth shall praise You with joyful lips." I shall overcome them and possess the gates of my enemies. No man shall be able to stand against me because Jehovah will put the fear of me upon them. They may come against me with swords, spears, and javelins but in the name of the Lord, I shall subdue them all. The siege upon my destiny is broken and I shall walk in total freedom. Nothing shall hinder me as I step into my place of glory and influence. **Amen.**

## CONFESSION

The Lord is my help in my times of trouble. I will not be afraid. God is my refuge and strength. I declare that he is my help when the troubles of life arise.

## Breakthrough Declaration 78

*Surely I will pour out my spirit on you; I will make my words known to you.*

*Proverbs. 1:23*

---

**H**eavenly Father, I nullify the plan of every demonic spirit and human agent seeking to destroy my life, my ministry, my business, marriage, family, career and everything else that concerns me or is connected to me in the name of Jesus. I nullify, cancel and veto the plans of every demonic spirit behind malicious gossip, lies, slander and accusation, spirit of jealousy, evil eye and envy which seeks to fight against my life without a cause in the name of Jesus. Let the sword of the Lord cut off the head of every snake and venomous spirit in the name of Jesus. Break the head of every python spirit in the Name of Jesus. Lord, preserve my life from the secret devices of the enemy. Hide me from the secret counsels of the enemy and guide my paths from falling into any satanic nets, traps and pits which the enemy has prepared for my feet in the name of Jesus. **Amen.**

### CONFESSION

My life is preserved from the snare of the fowler. No weapon formed against me will prosper in the Name of Jesus. The greater one lives inside of me. I am blessed.

## Breakthrough Declaration 79

*What shall we say about such wonderful things as these? If God is for us, who can ever be against us?*

*Romans 8:31*

---

**H**eavenly Father, I declare that if God is for me then no devil in hell can be against me. You have promised to be with me therefore no one will be able to stand against me. This is my year of possibilities. Every strongman or mountain in my life, I render you powerless and command you to fall and die under the power of God. I am blessed. I'm getting bigger, better and greater in Jesus Name. I decree and declare that He that is in me is greater than any force in the earth. I am protected on every side. The plans of the wicked shall not stand neither shall any evil befall my dwelling-place. The Lord is my shield and buckler. He shall give His angels charge over me, to keep me in all my ways. In their hands they shall bear me up, lest I dash my foot against a stone. **Amen.**

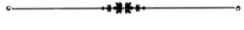

## CONFESSION

God is with me. No one can ever be against me. I declare that just as the Lord opened the Red Sea before Moses, He will cause me to drive away every obstacle that stands in my way. I declare that every flood lifted against me shall be silenced in the name of Jesus.

## Breakthrough Declaration 80

*Wait on the Lord: be of good courage, and he shall strengthen thine heart: wait, I say, on the Lord*

**Psalm 27:14**

---

**H**eavenly Father, I declare that I will wait upon the Lord for he has promised to strengthen my heart if I wait upon Him. I pray that the Holy Spirit would lay his mighty hands upon my life, expand my vision to see greater potentials and opportunities around me and to also enlarge my heart to believe bigger possibilities. Father, please empower me to do exceedingly, abundantly above all that I think or ask according to the Holy Spirit's power that works in me. Like Jabez, bless me and enlarge my territory, let your saving hand be upon me and my family. Prosper me everywhere the soles of my feet may touch in the mighty name of Jesus. **Amen.**

### CONFESSION

I declare, decree, pronounce, prophesy & speak into the atmosphere over the lives of myself & families that this is the acceptable year of the Lord. The portals of heavens are open over our lives, I decree and declare that we walk under an open heaven. We walk in the presence of God and in the supernatural glory of God.

## Breakthrough Declaration 81

*Let the wicked forsake his way, and the unrighteous man his thoughts: and let him return unto the Lord, and he will have mercy upon him; and to our God, for he will abundantly pardon.*

*Isaiah 55:7*

---

Heavenly Father, I command every assignment of the evil one to be broken over my life this year in the name of Jesus. I speak over my family, wife, husband, children, ministry, business, marriage, career, pastor, loved ones and everything else that concerns me or is connected to me and I command the assignment of the enemy to be broken over our health, finances, business, career, ministry, destiny and minds in the Name of Jesus Christ. I pray Father you release fire from heaven to uproot, destroy, nullify, cancel, shatter and annihilate every plan of the enemy concerning our lives in the mighty Name of Jesus Christ. I decree and declare that the anointing will force the devil to vomit what he stole from me in the Name of Jesus. **Amen.**

### CONFESSION

I declare that the enemy will not consume my family, business, marriage and children. I am covered by the blood of Jesus; therefore, the evil one cannot destroy my life.

## Breakthrough Declaration 82

*When you lie down, you will not be afraid;*
*when you lie down, your sleep will be sweet.*

*Proverbs 3:24*

---

**H**eavenly Father, I declare that I will not be afraid when I lie down to sleep. I declare that this year my sleep shall be sweet for the Lord gives his children perfect rest. I declare that you are the mighty God. You reign and rule victoriously over my life this year. I pray Lord that you establish Yourself in my life as wonderful, counsellor, the mighty God, the everlasting father, the Prince of Peace. I pray Lord that you take your rightful place in my life. Take your rightful place in my home, marriage, family, children, and ministry. Cause a wave of your anointing to flow in my life like never before. I consecrate and lay myself before You that Lord You would use me like never before. I lay aside everything in my life which does not glorify You and I declare that all I am and all that I have belongs to the King of Kings. Glorify Yourself in my life Lord. Let Your will be done and Your kingdom be established. **Amen.**

### CONFESSION

I have sweet sleep. I am free from worry, anxiety and insomnia. The Lord gives his children perfect sleep. The Lord reigns. The King of Glory reigns. He is Wonderful. The Counsellor reigns. The Mighty God reigns. The Everlasting Father reigns, The Prince of Peace reigns.

## Breakthrough Declaration 83

*So let's not get tired of doing what is good. At just the right time we will reap a harvest of blessing if we don't give up.*

*Galatians 6:9*

---

**H**eavenly Father, help me to never give up or quit in the work of the ministry. Though I might grow tired and weary I pray that You would give me the strength to persevere by the divine power of your grace and anointing. Thank You Lord that at the right time I will reap a harvest of blessing if I don't give up. I will arise and shine, for my light has come. The glory of God is risen upon me. Though darkness covers the earth, I am rising and I am shining. I am the light of the world therefore, I cannot be hidden. I am moving to a higher level and I occupy the place God has prepared for me. In this season, I am stretching out my boundaries. God is elevating me. By His Spirit, He beautifies my life and empowers me to do Greater Works. As I step into God's spotlight, I will be bigger, better and greater. He will perform new and unusual acts in my life. God's blessings come to me through unexpected ways and unusual people. He is bringing the right people my way.

## CONFESSION

I will not get tired of doing what is good. At the right time I will reap a harvest of blessing if I don't give up.

## Breakthrough Declaration 84

*When you pass through the waters, I will be with you; and through the rivers, they shall not overflow you. When you walk through the fire, you shall not be burned, nor shall the flame scorch you.*

*Isaiah 43:2*

Heavenly Father, when I pass through the waters, You have promised that You will be with me and the rivers shall not overflow me. When I walk through the fire, I shall not be burned, nor shall the flame scorch me. I declare that though the waters and storms of life arise I will not be afraid for the Lord is with me. I declare that though I walk through the fires of life, I will be safe from all calamity. A thousand may fall at my side, and ten thousand at my right hand; but it shall not come near me. No weapon formed against me and my destiny shall prosper. No evil shall come near my dwelling-place! For I am protected on every side! **Amen.**

## CONFESSION

I serve a God who is bigger than the storms and circumstances of life. God is with me and I will not be afraid. I will be still and know that You are God. The Lord my God has planted me like a tree by the waters. My roots are deep. My branches are wide. My fruits are marvelous. I am blessed beyond measure.

## Breakthrough Declaration 85

*I shall not die, but live, and declare the works of the LORD.*

*Psalm 118:17*

---

**H**eavenly Father, I declare according to Psalm 118:17, that I shall not die, but I shall live to declare the work of the Lord. I nullify every agenda of the spirit of death concerning my life and I command every assignment of the spirit of untimely death to be annihilated in the Mighty Name of Jesus Christ. I declare that this year no members of my family shall not die before our time in the Name of Jesus Christ. I declare my season of new beginnings is here, my breakthrough and total healing is here. My overflow is here. My uplifting and establishment is here and no man shall stand against me! I receive an expected overflow from the throne of God! The Lord has made room for me and I shall be fruitful in the land. **Amen.**

### CONFESSION

I shall not die but I will live to declare the glorious works of the Lord. Sickness, disease, untimely death, accidents and affliction shall not kill me before my time.

## Breakthrough Declaration 86

*Be strong and let your heart take courage,*
*All you who hope in the Lord.*

*Psalm 31:24*

**H**eavenly Father, I declare that I will be strong and my heart will take courage in You. I declare that my hope is in the Lord. I decree and declare that I am moving into divine purpose and acceleration to the next level of my life and destiny. Every door that has been wrongly closed will be opened in the name of Jesus. I declare that doors of healing, abundance, opportunity and favour are opened in the name of Jesus. I decree and declare that every opposition of the enemy is frustrated in the name of the Lord. Mountains will move before me. I am blessed with the blessing of the Lord. The Lord shall shut the mouth of every lion that rises against me. I will take courage and hope in the Lord. **Amen.**

## CONFESSION

My heart will take courage in the Lord for he is my hope and my strength. I decree and declare that every flood that is lifted up against me shall be silenced in the name of Jesus. I decree and declare that the ungodly floods of darkness shall not sweep over me.

## Breakthrough Declaration 87

*When a man's ways please the LORD, he maketh even his enemies to be at peace with him.*

*Proverbs 16:7*

---

**H**eavenly Father, Your word declares in Proverbs 16:7 that "when a man's way pleases the Lord, He makes even his enemies to be at peace with him." Therefore, I claim the peace of the Lord which surpasses all understanding. Lord, thank You that even in the midst of my enemies, You are causing my horn to be exalted and my cup to be running over. I decree and declare that this year every wall in my life which is standing as an opposition to the favour of God must come down in the name of Jesus. I command every Jericho wall standing as an obstacle to my breakthrough to be shattered in the name of Jesus. I command demonic walls of opposition, setback and adversity to be brought down in the Name of Jesus. I command every satanic blockade and resistance to be subdued in the mighty Name of Jesus. **Amen.**

## CONFESSION

There is no mountain bigger than my God. There is no power greater than my God. There is obstacle stronger than my God. There is no trial too difficult for my God. There is no opposition that can defeat my God.

## Breakthrough Declaration 88

*But as it is written: "Eye has not seen, nor ear heard, nor have entered into the heart of man the things which God has prepared for those who love Him."*

*1 Corinthians 2:9*

---

**H**eavenly Father, I pull down and nullify every assignment of Satan concerning my life, family, finances, business and children. I decree and declare that I am blessed and not cursed. I declare I am highly favored by the Lord and goodness and mercies shall follow me all the days of my life. I declare that God will raise me to be the envy of many. May the works of my hand and the fruit of my womb be blessed. May people go out of their way to bless me. I declare that I am not ordinary; I am a king, queen and a child of the Most High God. I decree and declare that this is my season of enlargement. I am experiencing God's abundant increase. The days of my small beginnings will turn around to a time of great abundance. I give God praise for my season of increase! **Amen.**

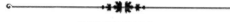

### CONFESSION

I decree and declare that the Lord will prepare a table for me in the presence of my enemies. I declare that my enemies and those who despise me will see the grace, mercy and favour of God over my life.

## Breakthrough Declaration 89

*Lord, by Your favor You have made my mountain stand strong.*

*Psalm 30:7*

---

Heavenly Father, I thank You that Your favor is causing my mountain to stand strong. I declare that this year Your favor is surrounding me like a shield and is going before me right now causing doors to be opened, mountains of opposition to be removed, finances and needs met, promotions granted, extraordinary acts of kindness, special privileges and advantages, divine increase and preferential treatment to be granted to me. Father I declare a divine season of accelerated breakthroughs in my life in the Name of Jesus. I command very blessing that the enemy has swallowed, to be coughed up and released in the Name of Jesus. My command my riches, money, house, land, miracles, business, children, destiny and every blessing which is rightfully mine to be released in this season in the Name of Jesus. I thank you Father that you are turning around everything in my favour even now in the Name of Jesus. I declare that this is my season of the divine turnaround in the Name of Jesus Christ.

## CONFESSION

I am walking into a season of breakthrough and accelerated promotion. I am a child of the King and declare the blessings of the Lord is evident upon my life.

## Breakthrough Declaration 90

*For You, O Lord, will bless the righteous; with favor You will surround him as with a shield.*

*Psalm 5:12*

---

**H**eavenly Father, I declare according to Psalm 5:12 "For You, O Lord, will bless the righteous; with favor You will surround him as with a shield." Lord, I thank You for the blessing and rich favor of the Lord which surrounds me as a shield. I declare I am blessed going in and blessed going out. I declare that my storehouses are blessed, bills are paid and debts are cleared because the favor of the Lord causes me to be the head and not the tail. I thank You that Your favor is overtaking me in all areas of my life. Thank You that the hand of God upon my life is causing me to be highly favored before men. Thank You for the blessing of the Lord. Lord, I declare divine favor over every area of my life. I declare it over my house, my family, business, marriage, ministry, children, grandchildren and their future generations. Thank You Lord that we shall be satisfied with Your favor and filled with Your blessings all the days of our lives.

### CONFESSION

I declare the favor of the Lord causes my years to be crowned with goodness and my paths filled with fatness in the Name of Jesus

## PRAYERS FOR FAVOR

It is the Lord's desire to bless you and cause his favor to shine upon you. Favor means "grace". The devil is against your uprising in life. As you declare these confessions may the favor of the Lord overtake you in life and cause you to be a blessing to those around you. From today your enemies will cry bitter tears because the favor of the Lord will locate you today.

---

❖ For You, O Lord, will bless the righteous; With favor You will surround him as with a shield. Psalm 5:12

❖ Lord, by Your favor You have made my mountain stand strong. Psalm 30:7

❖ Let them shout for joy and be glad, Who favor my righteous cause; And let them say continually, "Let the Lord be magnified, Who has pleasure in the prosperity of His servant." Psalm 35:27

- Father I thank you that I am blessed and highly favored. (Luke 1:28)
- I declare that I am crowned with glory and honor in the name of Jesus. (Psalm 8:5)
- Oh Lord I pray that this year you remember me and my family with your favor. Visit us I pray with your salvation. (Psalm 106:4)
- I declare this is the year of the favor of the Lord in the name of Jesus. (Isaiah 61:2)

- I declare this year I shall experience the favor of the Lord for this is my set time of favor in the name of Jesus. (Psalm 102:13)
- I declare that as a seed of Abraham, the favor of the Lord shall cause great increase to flow in my life. (Genesis 12)
- I declare that like Joseph I shall be favored in my career, business and above my peers in the name of Jesus. I declare that like Joseph the favor of the Lord shall cause promotion and increase to flow in my life in the name of Jesus. (Genesis 39)
- I declare that I am a covenant child of God therefore I enjoy the favor of the Lord
- I thank you Father, that your Word declares that I am the head and not the tail. I declare that the favor of God upon my life causes me to walk in abundant blessings.
- I declare that the blessings of the Lord makes me rich and adds no sorrows to it.
- Lord I pray that you position me at the right place and the right time to receive your divine favor.
- I declare that my horn shall be exalted because of your favor in the name of Jesus. (Psalm 89:17)
- I declare today that goodness and mercy shall accompany me all the days of my life in the name of Jesus. (Psalm 23:5-6)
- Lord I thank you that you daily load me with your favor and blessings.
- I declare that favor of the Lord surrounds me like a shield (Psalm 5:12)
- I declare that my enemies shall not triumph over me in the name of Jesus. I declare that I shall be like a mountain

which cannot be moved because of your divine favor in my life.

- I declare that the favor of the Lord shall cause my name to be great in the name of Jesus. (Exodus 11:3)
- I declare that I shall grow in stature and in favor with God and men. (1 Samuel 2:26)
- I declare that I shall have favor and high esteem in the sight of God and man in the name of Jesus. (Proverbs 3:4)
- I declare that the favor of the Lord is like the dew on the grass. I declare my life shall remain fruitful because the favor of the Lord causes me to walk in abundance, success and productivity. (Proverbs 19:12)
- I declare that I have good understanding in the name of Jesus.(Provers13:15)
- I declare that the favor of the Lord causes me to experience preferential treatment and special privileges in the name of Jesus.
- I declare that closed doors are opened because of the favor of the Lord. I declare that shut blessings are being released because of the favor of the Lord.
- I declare that I am blessed in the name of Jesus and every curse working against my favor in life is broken in the name of Jesus.
- I declare that the favor of the Lord causes my years to be crowned with goodness and my paths filled with fatness in the name of Jesus.

## PROSPERITY CONFESSIONS

"And he shall be like a tree planted by the rivers of water, that bringeth forth his fruit in his season; his leaf also shall not wither; and whatsoever he doeth shall prosper." Psalm 1:3

"For the Lord God is a sun and shield: the Lord will give grace and glory: no good thing will he withhold from them that walk uprightly." Psalm 84:11

- El Shaddai, I worship and honor you for you are the God of more than enough. You are the One who supplies all of my needs.
- I declare that you are my Jehovah Jireh the God who supplies all of my needs.
- I declare that in my prosperity I shall be like a mountain which cannot be moved in the name of Jesus. (Psalm 30:6)
- I declare that the wealth of the wicked shall be given to me in the name of Jesus. I declare that I shall enjoy the fruit of the land and I shall eat of the wealth of the Gentiles in the name of Jesus.
- Lord i thank you that you are my shield and my exceeding great reward. (Genesis 15)
- I declare that as I obey and serve the Lord, I will spend my days in prosperity and my years in pleasure. (Job 36:11)
- Oh Lord I pray send now prosperity (Psalm 118:25)
- I declare that I will eat the fruit of my labor; blessings and prosperity will be mine in the name of Jesus. (Psalm 128:2)
- I declare that with me are riches and honor, enduring wealth and prosperity. (Proverbs 8:18)

- I declare that the work of my hands will prosper in the name of Jesus. I declare prosperity upon my business, family and job in the name of Jesus.(Genesis 39:3)
- I declare that the Lord delights in my prosperity (Deut 28:63)
- Lord I thank you that you have given to me the power to get wealth for it is your covenant promise to me and my generations. (Deut 8:18)
- As I meditate on the Word of the Lord I declare that good success and prosperity is mine in the name of Jesus. (Joshua 1:8)
- I declare that as I seek the Lord. God will give me success in the name of Jesus. (2 Chronicles 26:5)
- I declare that my delight is in the Word of the Lord. I thank you Father that I am like a tree planted by the streams of water which yields its fruit in season. I declare that whatever I do prospers because the presence of the Lord is with me. (Psalm 1:2-3)
- I declare that goodness and mercy shall follow me all the days of my life (Psalm 23:6)
- I declare that I will not beg for bread in the name of Jesus. (Psalm 37:25)
- I declare that because I seek the Lord I will want no good thing. (Psalm 34:10)
- I shout for joy and declare Let the Lord be magnified who takes pleasure in my prosperity (Psalm 35:27)
- I declare that as I delight myself in the Lord he will grant me the desires of my heart. (Psalm 37:4)
- Lord I thank you that you have brought me to a place of rich abundance. (Psalm 66:12)

- Lord I thank you that wealth and riches are in my house and your righteousness endures forever (Psalm 112:3)
- I declare that as I pray for the peace of Jerusalem peace shall be within my walls and prosperity in my house. (Psalm 122:6-7)
- Because I fear the Lord and walk in his ways, I will eat the fruit of my labor and blessings and prosperity will be mine. I declare that my wife will be like a fruitful vine within my house and my children like olive shoots around my table in the name of Jesus. (Psalm 128:2-3)
- I declare that as I honor the Lord with my wealth and the first fruits of all my increase. My barns will be overflowing and my vats brim over with new wine. (Proverbs 3:9-10)
- I declare the blessings of the Lord brings wealth and he adds no sorrow to it. (Proverbs 10:22)
- I declare that as I am diligent in my work the Lord will bring increase in my life. I declare the ways of dishonesty I will not follow in the name of Jesus. (Proverbs 13:11)
- I declare that I will possess the wealth of the wicked in the name of Jesus. (Proverbs 13:22)
- I declare that the house of the righteous contains great treasure. (Proverbs 15:6)
- I commit to the Lord all my plans and I declare that I am prosperous (Proverbs 16:3)
- I declare that as I tithe and give offerings to the Lord. The windows of heaven are open over me, and the rain of the Lord fills my life with abundance that there is not room enough to contain it. I thank you father that you have promised to rebuke the devour for my sake and all nations

shall call me blessed in the name of Jesus. (Malachi 3:10-12)

- I declare that my God will supply all of my needs according to his riches in glory in Christ Jesus. (Philippians 4:19)
- I pray Father that you help me to prosper in all things and to be in health even as my soul prospers. (3 John 1:2)

Made in United States
Orlando, FL
15 March 2022

15772213R30059